T0146621

KNOCK OUT LIBERALISM AND KEEP OUR COUNTRY STRONG FOR ALL
AMERICANS

R.T. BROWN

KNOCK OUT LIBERALISM AND KEEP OUR COUNTRY STRONG FOR ALL AMERICANS

iUniverse books may be ordered through booksellers or by contacting:

iUniverse
1663 Liberty Drive
Bloomington, IN 47403
www.iuniverse.com
1-800-Authors (1-800-288-4677)

ISBN: 978-1-5320-6550-7 (sc)
ISBN: 978-1-5320-6551-4 (e)

Print information available on the last page.

iUniverse rev. date: 03/20/2019

Contents

What I Bring to the Table

I am a political analyst who has conservative views and has a goal to expose the democrats desire to control the lives of Americans. I go back to President Lyndon Johnson and the election of 1968 between Hubert Humphrey and Richard Nixon and all elections that have followed.

My reading material and research goes from the far left to the far right and all in between. I take pride in listening to all views and to call out my side when I think they are incorrect. I admit to making mistakes in life and I am always ready to share my triumphs and mistakes with others.

This is a book about the Republican Party and how we can win over the great percentage of the American People! There will be no spin allowed and nothing but facts and the truth! There will be no harsh talk just plain information that will bring many voters to our side. The liberal part of the democrat party will be shaking in their boots and there will be nothing they can do as we go forward in our mission for the American People! You will see we are hard hitting and full of great information and solutions!

Summary

I am looking for fellow patriots who want to be leaders and supporters! So get involved and make a difference for millions of Americans.

Bob Brown

I follow three rules: Do the right thing, do the best you can, and always show people you care.

Lou Holtz

We all have to Come Together for a Better America

My definition of coming together is our side uniting to defeat the liberal wing of the Democratic Party. Our team consists of The Tea Party, Conservatives, Moderates, Rinos, Establishment, and Left of Center. We will all unite for the benefit of our country, and we will respect each other's opinion.

The prime example of dividing our side was the presidential primaries of 2016. We all know there was a lot of mudslinging and personal insults during the primaries. I will not rehash the problems, but it must never happen again. We turned against each other and it gave Clinton and the democrats an opening to win.

We have primarily the same goals but perhaps some different paths of travel. Our discussions will be civil and strictly among ourselves! There will be no personal attacks and leaks to the media. We will be classified as family and will act as such. All families have some controversies and the proper way to handle the issues is to keep a lid on it.

The ultimate goal is with facts; truth and history to increase the percent of people who claim to be conservatives. This can be done and we will accomplish our goals.

Summary

Our ability to keep our family together is imperative to our success and future political victories! The media and the liberals will do their best to break up our family and we must fend them off.

People who work together will win, whether it be against complex football defenses, or the problems of modern society.

Vince Lombardi

The Strength of Liberalism in America

Liberalism took hold in the Lyndon Johnson presidency and has grown through the years. This was the beginning of The Great Society, and the start of dependence on the government. President Johnson and the Democrats thought that by giving benefits to people, it would create a person that would be motivated to get off of the public dole.

Liberalism since the mid sixty's has been looked upon as being hip and cool. It has been glorified by the Hollywood elite and has been made mainstream by The Big Three (as will be discussed in detail in the next chapter.)

Polls have shown the growth of liberalism and the hooks it has on different segments of our society. For years we were mainly 40% conservative, 36% moderate and about 20% liberal. I have always doubted these stats but there was always a consistency.

The polls and society is flowing to the left and the liberals understand this and are reloading. I have studied polls, demographics, housing patterns, education, and so much more. This is not the time to gloat but the time to put the hammer down on the liberals and make them irrelevant!

Summary

It is a must to stop the growth of liberalism and to stop it fast in it tracks! Our plan once organized will be the nail in the coffin as long as we govern correctly from now on.

That is one reason "feelings" and "compassion" are two of the most often used liberal terms. "Character" is no longer a liberal word because it implies self-restraint. "Good and evil" are not liberal words either as they imply a moral standard beyond one's feelings. In assessing what position to take on moral or social questions, the liberal asks him or herself, "How do I feel about it?" or "How do I show the most compassion?" — Not "What is right?" or "What is wrong?" For the liberal, right and wrong are dismissed as unknowable, and every person chooses his or her own morality.

Dennis Prager

The Big Three (Media, Academia, and the Hollywood Elite)

The Big Three has been a needle in the side of conservatives for a long time. We have always acted like a barking dog with no bite, but it is our time to bite and bring millions of Americans to our side. I am simply tired of us sitting on our hands and not acting for the American People!

I bet you are curious about what or who is The Big Three? They have been indoctrinating our young people, controlling the media and doing their best to stop conservative free speech. We are going to rattle the cages of The Media, Academia, and The Hollywood Elite. I can't wait to get us organized and in an attack mode and also I can't wait to see the liberal heads spin!

This will be our niche and we will go full speed ahead and expose the liberals for what they are. We will be protesting, boycotting, and rattling a lot of cages. We have allowed the liberals to rule for too long and it is now our time to inform Americans what the liberals have done and what they have planned for the future.

Media has been the mouthpiece of the liberals for a long time. All you need to do is watch CNN, MSN, NBC and all the other outlets and the obvious bias for the liberals.

Academia is a real mess and getting worse every day as we sit on our hands and gripe! This is the breeding ground of liberalism and where they have a strong presence of liberal professors. Liberal professors outnumber conservatives by 5 to 1 and it is probably a higher number of liberals.

The Hollywood Elite has a lot of power with the big screen and TV shows which are slanted to the far left. The platform for actors gives them the big stage to deliver their liberal views to America and the world. We will expose the ignorance of these people with facts and the truth.

Summary

The Big Three are totally out of control and is doing a lot of harm to our country. They are dumping their liberal agenda on Americans and they are the mouth pieces for liberalism! We have the plan to expose and stop this aggression and bring millions of people to our side. This is our niche and we will be aggressive in defeating the liberal views with facts and the truth. Next chapter we are going to start to get into the nuts and bolts with Citizen Leaders.

Repetition does not transform a lie into a truth."

Franklin D. Roosevelt

Citizen Leaders All Over America

The citizen leaders are the nuts and bolts of our organization as we go forward. They will help with organizing protests, boycotting and phone calls on issues that we find that need to be addressed.

There are many issues that we will be active on and we will rattle some cages! No more sitting on the porch and griping; it is time to take action. The Big Three, Media, Academia, and The Hollywood Elite are a major problem and I am personally very tired of our side getting slapped around all the time. It is time for us to be proactive and to counter attack some of the liberal nonsense.

We will have boots on the ground all over the country, working for the common cause. We will have regional, state, and community leaders. There will be many supporters and advocates that will stand with us.

Our citizen leaders will be known to the politicians in their areas and they will be operating in a professional manner. Our people will always take the high road but we will not be bullied and at times will rattle some cages.

Everybody involved with Conservative Wisdom United is very important to our cause and everyone can be an active part in one way or another. This can be with protesting, boycotts, and phone calls. You may also choose to be silent and just make donations to our cause.

Summary

Our goals are very important and it is all tied together for our cause. The organizing of our leaders and others down the line will take some time and we all have to be patient. It is important for us to grow and to be represented all over the country. I will need a lot of help from everybody to find the best people for all of the positions that will need to be filled.

Coming together is a beginning; keeping together is progress; working together is success.

Henry Ford

This is How We Will Spend Our Money on Billboards

I must say, I love Billboards! Our program will be very successful by just using them the correct way! But we have so much more to offer America.

We will be very honest, direct and persuasive with our billboards. We are going to venture into areas most Republicans have little desire to go to earn votes. Conservative Wisdom United will with help from our leaders and supporters, go into these areas and inform the citizens what the democrats have planned and are doing to Americans!

The Billboards will be factual and truthful, and with the help from our other tools we will reach our goals of earning 20% of the Black and the majority of the Latino vote by 2020! I am extremely excited about what we will accomplish with the help of millions of Americans!

We will be big and bold in our print and the people will notice!

Here are some examples of Billboards in our big cities:

Crime and Poverty out of Control! Who has been in charge of STL for over 50 years? Democrats! That's who! Vote Republican for a better way of life!

Vote Republican for a better way of life!! The democrats are using Black People for their vote! Check out this information. Links with more information!

Are you happy with your living conditions? Why are you voting democrat and allowing them to herd and corral you! Vote Republican for freedom and a better way of life!

We can be very creative with our Billboards and we will get people thinking!

I will also be working with Blacks who are Republicans and we will have Black Leaders in the Black communities dropping flyers, town halls and so much more!

Summary

I am very excited about our billboard plan and the great potential to educate others and to bring more voters to our side! I need a lot of help, donations, leaders, supporters, enthusiasm, and so much more for a better America for all of its citizens.

Republicans believe in equal opportunity and the democrats believe in equal results

Bob Brown

How Do We Earn the Black Vote

This is a huge challenge but we are up to it and we will succeed! This battle will be tough because of The Big Three and the liberals. The Black folks have been pandered to and lied to by the Democrats for a long time, all for the almighty vote.

The Republicans are at fault for failing to speak the truth and also being scared of The Big Three! We are going to blow the lid off the pot and the Democrats will shiver in despair!

We will be recruiting Conservative Black Folks all across America to be leaders and supporters. I hope to get some Black heavy hitters on board with us to give us more credibility. This will not be an easy chore and we need to have patience. We have to be honest with the fact that there are a lot of Black People that are under the spell of the Democrats and no matter what we do they will not leave them.

We have a lot of ammunition with our leaders, billboards, town halls, Conservative Black Leaders and so much more!

My goal is for the Republicans to earn 20% of the Black Vote by 2020. This is a reasonable goal because Conservative Wisdom United will be exposing the Democrats desire to control people and to keep them stupid.

Summary

We will be promoting Conservative views and lifestyle. We have been allowing the Democrats to carry the ball for so long and all we do is chase or stand still! No more Mr. nice guy with the liberal's eagerness to control and keep Black People under their Democrat tent.

Obstacles don't have to stop you. If you run into a wall, don't turn around and give up. Figure out how to climb it, go through it, or work around it.

Michael Jordon

How Do We Earn the Latino Vote

My goal by 2020 is for the Republicans to earn more than half of the Latino vote! If we get people aboard to work our program and use all of our tools, we will be successful. There is no doubt in my mind that we should have very solid support from this community!

We will go out and recruit conservative Latinos who want to be leaders and active in their community. We then get our other leaders and supporters into the Latino communities with flyers, town halls, and speaking the truth with solid facts. We hit businesses and pound on doors to get our information out.

We will be heavy with our Billboard program and hit the Democrats hard and expose their dastardly deeds! Our Billboards will be bold and they will knock the Democrats dizzy and promote the views and lifestyle of hard working Republicans.

I am really excited about what we will do with the Latino communities all across America! There is no doubt they should be on our side because they are hard workers and they have a desire to better themselves.

Summary

This Community is very important to America because of their growth in our country. We want to really work and explain to them the advantage of voting Republican and being a conservative. I really like this group because they are hard working and they are very good natured people! We will bring the Latinos to our side and this will cause the Democrats heads to spin!

Don't measure yourself by what you have accomplished, but by what you should have accomplished with your ability.

John Wooden

The Great American Discussion Group

As we grow this will be very important, but it will take time to recruit speakers and fill our territories. This will need to be very organized like our leaders and we will need a lot of help. It would be to our advantage to get some heavy hitters but if we don't we can create our own big dogs.

We want to have a group of speakers in all states that will expose the liberals and promote our Conservative views. Each group will contain between 5-8 speakers from different fields. They will speak about their field and what it takes to be an American. They will talk about hard work, dedication and they will all be motivators!

I saw a man and woman a couple of years ago dressed as Colonialist. They came in front of our group and they were awesome! They went through the Declaration of Independence and were very impressive! They are on board with us and will be awesome!

We will also talk about what it means to be a conservative and the opportunities it brings for all Americans. We will also expose the liberal's plan for Americans to be stupid and under control all for their vote.

Summary

When this is up and going it will make a huge difference in many communities. But it will take involvement and we need to get a lot of people stepping up to the plate, to be speakers, but to also refer others.

Socialism is a philosophy of failure, the creed of ignorance, and the gospel of envy, its inherent virtue is the equal sharing of misery.

Winston Churchill

Protest Colleges and Schools

Republicans have allowed the Big Three to rule and the prime example is our school system! It is a haven of liberalism that is inflicting damage on our young people and creating future problems. Conservative Wisdom United and the Republican Party will go to battle to defeat this out of control disease at its roots.

We will work to have student leaders and groups that are supporters of Conservative Wisdom United. They will keep us informed on issues that are not appropriate. When we determine there are problems, we will have our student association and local members take action.

There will be a discussion on what action to take and believe me, there will be action! We will make an appointment with the chancellor if needed or to go directly to a professor. There may be a need for protesting and counter protesting. The media will be informed about what we are doing and if they ignore us, they will be protested! In other words we are no longer sitting on the porch and griping, but we are rattling the cages of The Big Three.

Summary

The political correctness in our universities is completely out of control and Conservative Wisdom United is ready to get after it! We will be united in our effort to expose and defeat liberalism in our schools. We will be watching from kindergarten all the way up the ladder to our universities. We are going after liberalism on many fronts and they will be defeated!

The most fundamental fact about the ideas of the political left is that they do not work. Therefore we should not be surprised to find the left concentrated in institutions where ideas do not have to work in order to survive.

Thomas Sowell

Democrats and the Big City Failures

The big cities are the Achilles Heel of the Democrat party! This is where the rubber meets the pavement. This is where the Democrats are weak, and guess what; we are going to pounce on this subject for the American people.

How is it possible for the Democrats to keep winning elections in our big cities? I know what the answer is, The Big Three. Then you throw in lying, pandering, using and narcissism.

What first comes to your mind when you think of a city like St. Louis, Chicago, and Detroit? You guessed it, crime, drugs, lack of fathers, and a lot of people that lack knowledge. Some may say, "Bob Brown you are a little harsh". I say to those folks, that some people are content with lies instead of the difficult truth. I will always get to the point in a professional manner and will not skirt the issue.

We are going to expose what the Democrats have been doing to our big cities! This will be done with our leaders, supporters, and billboards. Some of the areas will have our foot soldiers going to businesses and having town hall meetings.

We will inform the media about our plans and they will report our actions or they will be protested.

Summary

This issue will be handled in a couple of different ways. There is the work that gets done in the circle and outside the circle. In the circle has been stated and I will give a quick synopsis of outside the circle.

The people who live in the suburbs and rural areas will hear loud and clear what the democrats have done to the big cities. The Democrats will be exposed and will not have a leg to stand on!

There is no question that liberals do an impressive job of expressing concern for blacks. But do the intentions expressed in their words match the actual consequences of their deeds?

Thomas Sowell

Fundraisers for Republicans and have Part Going to Charities

This idea will keep Republicans in the news all over America. Conservative Wisdom United will donate money to charities under our name and as Republicans. Our leaders will confer and we will find the charities that we will support. We will not give our money out blindly but will give it to organizations or people that are go getters and who believe in a strong and prosperous America. This could be entrepreneurs, health, education, and charities that help people in need.

I would love to see our political and citizen leaders visit children in hospitals and bring some joy to their lives. Visit retirement homes and talk with the elderly and the staff. When you are home in your district, just drive around and go into businesses and talk with the people and let them know you are there to help them help themselves.

Republican politicians (leaders) have to be in the public eye and making appearances as much as possible. This is a full time job not a country club to get together with the elites! Your job is to be with the people in your community and to always be within reach. Our leaders from the top, down to the organizers are people persons who are always in the active and social mode.

Summary

We are Conservative Republicans and we believe in the power of the people and not the big controlling government. We are constantly in the motivating mode at all times and this is very obvious to our constituents! I am always in the teaching and motivating gear to help others to help themselves, to be better people. I will expect this from all of our political and citizen leaders from the top down to our supporters.

A man never stands as tall as when he kneels to help a child.

The Knights of Pythagoras

What is a Liberal and What are Their Goals to Control Americans

The liberal politicians will never admit to errors in their philosophy of what is best for our country. They are narcissistic and they refuse to look in the mirror.

All they want in life is to control people and to keep them uninformed, ignorant and stupid. Wiki leaks proved this a fact that a lot of us have known for many years.

The liberals want to be the cowboys herding and corralling Americans all for the power. A lot of Americans have been fooled over the last fifty years with the democrats and thinking they want the best for the people.

There is not a government big enough and spends enough for the liberals. The more the government spends the more control they have of the people. The liberal politicians are all about control and what they need to do to keep their lifestyle.

I'll bet when they are in their special groups of people they trust they are talking and making disparaging remarks about fellow Democrats. Hillary Clinton is a prime example of the Queen Bee and all below her are just people to use for her benefit. Clinton and her treatment of people she thinks are under her is a disgrace!

Summary

I separate the liberals from Democrats, because we can bring a lot of hard working Democrats to our side with the facts and the truth. The Democrats will be doing their best to keep their base and controlling The Big Three! They will do whatever it takes to keep the Blacks and Latinos in line for their support and will degrade us for our honesty.

Republicans believe in personal responsibility, small government, and a strong military, while the liberals believe the opposite!

Republicans believe in equal opportunity and the liberals believe in equal results!

We are going to expose the liberals at every corner all across America and we will defeat them for a better America for all of its citizens.

Life in general has never been even close to fair, so the pretense that the government can make it fair is a valuable and inexhaustible asset to politicians who want to expand government.

Thomas Sowell

How to Persuade Voters to Our Side with Facts and the Truth

This is extremely important and this will work from President Trump, Republican Politicians, Citizen Leaders, Republican Supporters, and Conservative Wisdom United Supporters.

I see many problems on both sides with people getting angry and turning to personal insults. The prime example was the Republican Primary and the general election of 2016.

Social media is full of people that are downright nasty and vile! I see it all the time coming from both sides. I have always felt that we had more character and class than the liberals, but I am now worrying we are going into the sewer with them. We all need to step it up and concentrate on being persuasive to bring more people to our side.

Conservative Wisdom United will take the high road at all times and will expect all that are involved with us to do the same. We will have lively debates and we will always be civil in our actions.

I will go into depth on the art of persuasion writing and communicating when we get to our strategy. In the meantime I will give a couple of examples that I used to our advantage. The main objective is to know your subject and have confidence in your delivery. Stay calm, listen to your audience and show interest.

I met a college student from Iraq and we got along very well discussing his country and culture, (I love talking to people from other states and countries to learn about their values and the makeup of their country.)

The subject of the 2012 election came up after discussing the politics of Iraq and the Middle East. He said that Syria was not a terrorist nation! I listened intently to his points and then I firmly and professionally disagreed with him and gave him some information.

He said he was not eligible to vote but he had friends and they all voted for Obama. I asked him why they supported Obama and his response was that he is for the people. I asked him, "are you a good student?" to which he replied proudly that he is an A student.

I looked at him straight in the eyes and said, "for example there are 5 students that make straight A's and they are constantly at home studying and preparing themselves for a prosperous future. They very rarely go out and they don't get involved in the beer drinking scene."

"Another 5 students are always out drinking beer and staying out late. They are not studying and thinking about their future, but have the women and beer on their mind. They are neglecting their studies and voila', they received D's and F's on their report card."

"The University President called all ten of the guys into his office and they discussed their grades. The president is pacing back and forth and then he comes up with this solution. Why don't we take the students with the A grades and the students with the bad grades and average them out, and everybody will receive C's?"

I asked him "does that sound fair to you?" He replied, "no way; I do not want to share my grades with the others because I worked hard to make these grades!"

My next sentence was, "this is what the Democrats are trying to do in our country. Republicans believe in equal opportunity and the Democrats believe in equal results."

There was some more political banter between us and when I left he was very happy to have met me and for the information. He said he understood a lot more about the issues and will share this with his friends.

Another guy I met who had a wife and two kids and I could tell he was not well off. He started talking about the rich Republicans and how the Democrats are for the little guy. I listened to what he had to say and I noticed in his car that he had a rifle. I told him that the NRA is always in support of the Republican Party. I asked him, "are you an NRA member?" He said he darn sure was and has been for years. Do you realize that if the democrats had all the power in the government we would lose the second amendment?

I explained to him the desire for the Democratic Party is to herd and control people all for their vote.

After our discussion and listening to him and giving him solutions to his problems, I am confident he will come to our side of freedom!

We have to listen to the concerns of others and deliver the solutions. We can all do this to a degree and be successful.

Summary

I will have a lot of great information on this in our strategy EBook that will help build our Super Pac. This is just one of our many tools for a Great America for all Americans! We will all work hard for our ultimate goal of leaving a better country for our children and grandchildren!

Let us be sure that those who come after will say of us in our time, that in our time we did everything that could be done. We finished the race; we kept them free; we kept the faith.

Ronald Reagan

Be a Trusted Mentor for Others Who Don't Have Interest or Time to Research Issues

Being a mentor is advantageous to our cause because there are many people on both sides that need the information that we are all sharing. We will have an information pipeline that everybody will be using in our organization. I am an information junkie and I know we have a lot of people that are the same. Our mentors will be able to use this information to bring others to our side with our usage of persuasion.

There are many people in our country who are misinformed or don't take the time to research subjects or just don't care. These people are our targets and they range from left of center to the conservatives. Anybody that is further to the left than left of center is probably a lost cause to come to our side.

I talk to people all the time that don't see what is going on and they can be on our side. Some people run businesses or work a lot of hours or prefer to spend their time with family or recreation.

First thing you can do is to get people involved at minimal as donators, so they can receive our newsletter. This is a good start or you can just pop in with information periodically.

We can be a person of knowledge on subjects in our office, work place and business. In high schools and colleges strive to be the informed one that can explain the issues in a smart, persuasive way to others.

We have to as mentors, gain the trust of others in order for them to view us as an authority. Listening and doing research is the answer and we can all do a better job of that.

The number one concern of our mentors is the people we want to bring to our side with our knowledge. They will need to understand that they will always hear the facts and truth from us at all times.

Summary

Always be positive and never get into a shouting match with others. Do not be a ranter that is all mouth and no substance. Always state the facts and truth and let the chips fall where they may.

Always be prepared with articles, statistics and links to share, and after a while you will build an audience and will have a lot of respect from others. After a while you can say that you read this or saw that and then go about your business.

I receive information from the far left and the far right, because I want to know what the liberals are doing so I can strategize for Conservative Wisdom United and the Republican Party. I will share articles and information like it is going out of style!

You need to understand that some people will say things that make no sense. They will be angry with their words and your instincts will tell you to let them rant and you just go on your way.

The main job for our mentors is to report the news to people who are uninformed, or who don't have the time to research. You want to be the source that others look to and respect.

Alone we can do so little; together we can do so much.

Helen Keller

Duplication is Our Key to Reach Our Goals for America

I have set our goals high, but they are attainable with our good team. I am counting on each and every one of you to step up in some capacity to help us all to be successful. Once our two Super PAC books, Knock Out Liberalism and Keep Our Country Strong for All Americans and The Strategy That Will Cause the Democrats to Panic are absorbed, I will make it very easy to duplicate out to Facebook friends, and other social media. With friends, neighbors and acquaintances there is another easy way to promote Conservative Wisdom United.

We will have a marketing link with different pieces that can be downloaded and all that you will have to do is insert your name or just copy and share. This will be included when you sign in on our website.

You will need to post some of this information on your Facebook page periodically. I would love to see everybody share this one time on messenger. It will be real simple but it will take some time, depending on the number of friends you want to message. Plus any other social media you are involved with, please share our information.

There will be several flyers that you can download and share with people on the street or social media.

Summary

Our people are very important to help us grow our organization to expose the liberal agenda. It is important to have fun and stay focused on our target of a better America for all of its citizens! Set your goals and share and talk about what we are going to accomplish for our children and grandchildren. What we are doing will go down in our history books as an organization that stepped up to the plate and hit a home run!

Goal – We have our goals of 20% of the Black and the majority of the Latino vote by 2020!

Conservative Manifesto

A Conservative Manifesto involves these core principles:

1. Personal responsibility, small government, and a strong military

2. Education, intelligence, and independent thinkers

3. Fathers and the family

4. Concern for others and help those that want to help themselves

5. Equal opportunity and not equal results

6. Encourage others at all times

7. Honesty, character and hard work

8. Leaders that are bold and speak the truth

9. The desire to succeed and to make a difference

10. Energy independence – use all resources

11. Seal the borders

12. Expose the democrats

13. We need all Conservative Americans to step up and get after it

14. Get liberals out of our schools

15. We will not be scared to speak the truth

16. Speak out loudly against corruption

17. Push to be your best everyday

18. Be active and understand the issues in our country and around the world

19. Share your knowledge of issues and bring more voters to the Conservative Republican Party

20. We will not allow the liberals to indoctrinate our youth and fellow Americans

21. Volunteer for our cause

22. The Republican Party will be watched like a hawk and will be called out when they stray

23. Discuss the benefits of being a Conservative

24. Stress Conservative Republicans is a lifestyle and a year round plan

25. We are in a battle against the liberals

26. Give our children love and discipline

27. Jealousy is a bad word, instead use envious

28. Dream of success for your family and country

29. We will not be porch people and sit on our hands

30. America will not have the problems of the democrat run big cities

31. Protest the liberal media

Freedom is never more than one generation away from extinction. We didn't pass it to our children in the bloodstream. It must be fought for, protected, and handed on for them to do the same.

Ronald Reagan

Republican Politicians, We Refer to as Republican Leaders will Strive for our Endorsement

I can't stand the word politician, it makes my skin crawl! No more politicians on our side talking out of both sides of their mouth. We want people in our organization that will use their head and have a heart.

As we progress and the Republican Leaders see the value of a relationship with Conservative Wisdom United, they will then want our endorsement. We will earn this with honesty and doing business with integrity and class. This is the road we will travel and there will be no getting off the pavement.

In return we will only endorse candidates who have high ethical standards and whom are real Conservatives. There will be consistency in their beliefs and the understanding that not all Americans will be fond of them. You have enemies? Good. That means you've stood up for something, sometime in your life. (Winston Churchill) They will understand the benefit of working with our state directors and leaders and are proud to have an association with Conservative Wisdom United.

Summary

Character and doing what is right is expected from all of our people and we will not stray! We will always carry ourselves with dignity in public and will be firm and under control with the opposition. We know the opposition is liberalism and there will be times that the heat will be turned up. When this happens they will take notice and will know we mean business!

We can all be successful and make money, but when we die, that ends. But when you are significant is when you help other people be successful. That lasts many a lifetime.

Lou Holtz

Conservative Wisdom United Informative Ezine and Website

Everybody who comes on and purchases our (Knock Out Liberalism and Keep Our Country Strong for All Americans and become members of Conservative Wisdom United and receive our strategy book (The Strategy That Will Cause the Democrats to Panic!) will be on our mailing list for informational emails and our ezine. This is where news will be shared from our website about protests, town halls, video testimonials, newly appointed leaders, articles, and any other news worthy events.

Our blog will be a great recruiting tool to grow our organization and the Republican Party. All we need to do is get the potential member to our site and they will be very impressed! They will see we are loaded with great information and a lot of video testimonials.

We are going to do our best to be a motivating factor in many lives. This is of the utmost of importance to me personally. I want people to reach their personal goals and to be the best they can be! I love the faces of people who have been working real hard and are near or have reached some goals. Conservative Wisdom United will be a motivator and cheerleader for people who desire to have a better life for themselves, family and those around them!

Summary

We are going to have the liberals shaking in fear as we work our tails off to have the people in control. Americans will have information that will bring millions to our side and the Democrats will be made irrelevant. Everybody needs to use our duplication process and take advantage of our website!

I never learn anything talking. I only learn things when I ask questions.

Lou Holtz

Conservative Wisdom United Will Be a Leader in Motivating Americans

Moving forward as a country it is important to be honest with our fellow citizens. Part of that is to expect everybody to be the best they can be, and for them to hopefully work towards reaching their goals in life.

A part of being a motivator is to be a good role model and to always look to do the right thing. Children and young people are very impressionable and can copy what they see. I have always stressed honesty, character and hard work -- you need to have all three.

We all need to be motivators for our families but also to others we have just met or strangers. I am constantly motivating others to do their best every day.

A direct way to be a motivator is to be a teacher or an athletic coach. They are very important in the lives of young people and they can make a difference.

We will have billboards that will be motivational all over the country! There will be donations and awards to those that are busting their tails!

Our state directors and citizen leaders will be encouraging everybody to give their best every day.

Summary

I have always believed that each generation was supposed to learn from the previous, the pitfalls and the triumphs! This is not being done as much as it should, as our character and culture is taking a beating.

I am talking about our personal and work life and how things are not going in the right direction. I see it every day and I am really hoping we can motivate people to raise their expectations as we go forward.

Conservative Wisdom United has goals that will benefit all Americans and we need everybody to jump aboard for America!

Ability is what you're capable of doing. Motivation determines what you do. Attitude determines how well you do it.

Lou Holtz

Democrats are Intentionally Keeping People Under Control

Some of us have known this as a fact for a real long time. Now we have proof with the Wiki leaks Democrat emails. Why, may I ask, are Democrats in favor of expanding the size of government? They want as many people as possible to be receiving checks from Uncle Sam. This is what they have been doing for over 50 years and we are now seeing the outcome.

We are going to plaster on billboards all across America the desire of the Democratic Party to keep Americans stupid and under control! They will be exposed for all to see and this will be something we can do right away! We will bring millions of Democrats to our side and all the Democratic Party will have left is the out-of-touch liberals!

Summary

It is very important for the electorate to understand the liberal mind and their desire to control our lives. We will be leading the way and we will be successful in exposing the liberals desire to keep Americans Stupid and under Control!

That's the definition of 'success' for the modern Democrat Party. As many people dependent on government as possible is the objective.

Rush Limbaugh

The Growth of Socialism in America

I know people that are Republicans or Conservatives that say we won the 2016 election by a landslide and that we have dominated down ballot the last 8 years. The former is correct about the last 8 years, but the 2016 election was not a landslide for Trump.

The democrats are reloading and plotting what they can do to derail the train. They are a very political bunch and are constantly thinking how they can fool the American People!

Besides The Big Three and counting on the Black and Latino vote, they have Socialism. There have been two gallop polls over the last 5-6 years that state that half the democrats hold a favorable view of Socialism. Further, consider the popularity of Bernie Sanders and his socialist agenda.

His strength is with the millennial and promoted with enthusiasm by our universities. A survey, taken at the end of January, 2016 found that 43 percent of Americans under 30 had a favorable view of Socialism.

Summary

As you can see we have our work cut out for us and it is time to turn this around. We are going to be aggressive on many fronts with billboards, citizen leaders and so much more!

The inherent vice of capitalism is the unequal sharing of blessings; the inherent virtue of socialism is the equal sharing of miseries.

Winston Churchill

What Would Happen If the Democrats Had Complete Control?

Just imagine the presidency and both houses in complete control by the Democrats for say, 12 years. We can't do much but gripe as America slips away. I will go through the scenario and what the outcome would be for Americans.

Conservative Wisdom United will not allow this to happen because we are going into high gear to defeat the liberals and expose their evil.

I will go into more detail, but if you want to cut to the skinny, just look at our big cities. Almost all of them have been democratic controlled for over 50 years! The crime, housing, education, lack of fathers and families is rampant. Most are like war zones and the people still support the Democratic Party?

This will be a short synopsis, but I think you will get the idea.

Well let's start with entitlements and how the democrats reeled in the voters by getting more Americans Dependent on the government. The cost of entitlements will go up and guess who will pay more? You guessed it, the successful producers will be overly taxed and they will lose their desire to make more money and to expand their businesses.

The military will be gutted and the rules of engagement will make it impossible for us to shoot first. Guess what, nobody wants to enlist into the liberal military.

Law enforcement will have their hands tied even more by the Democrats and PC police. Crime expands and it moves even more to the suburbs and rural areas. People decide not to go into law enforcement so the liberals lower the standards to bring in people you don't want to be in the same room with.

Housing and urban development department will start moving the urban people with their problems to the suburbs and rural areas. This will expand the crime and bad schools to previously nice areas.

I think you get the idea!

Summary

Conservative Wisdom United and millions of hard working and patriotic Americans will never let this happen! We need to act now and not later. We need to expose and make the Democratic Party irrelevant and also give The Big Three a thrashing!

Liberals talk about the 'income inequality' and the 'unfairness' and the disparity of the haves and the have-nots in New York City. Who has been running that city for all this time? Who has created the underclass in this country? It's the Democrat Party.

Rush Limbaugh

Republican National Strategy Plan

This is something that should have been done a long time ago! This will be similar to the Contract with America from 1994. Contract with America was a campaign plan and what we have is a 365 day a year lifestyle! Our Book (Knock Out Liberalism and Keep Our Country Strong for All Americans) is our guide and (The Strategy That Will Cause the Democrats to Panic!) is the strategy!

We will start at the top with our presidential candidates. I am with President Reagan and the belief of "thou shall not speak ill of any fellow Republican."

The Republican Primary of 2016 was a disgrace and should never be repeated. We need to be civil to each other and respectfully disagree on issues and always take the high road. The personal insults to other candidates and individuals were terrible and very immature.

We want candidates up and down the ticket to have strong character and are leaders and not so called politicians. The Republican's problem is lack of leadership and not thinking of the people they serve. They need to speak the truth with facts and not to try to please everyone.

We want Republicans to come on board with Conservative Wisdom United and sign an agreement to be a part of our organization and the National Strategy Plan. They can use this as ammunition against the liberals. There will be guidelines, rules and an ethics clause that will need to be followed.

Conservative Wisdom United will promote our candidates by state and nationally. We will push our Republican billboards all over America and will stress to vote straight Republican up and down the ticket. The Republicans will have the full force of Conservative Wisdom United exposing the democrats and promoting the views and lifestyle of conservative Republicans with our many tools. We will push the Republican brand as a group all across America.

Summary

An example, say for Missouri would be, with all of our billboards, leaders, supporters and our full arsenal promote the Republican Party of Missouri 365 days of the year! Now of course we will be extremely heavy in the typical campaign season.

We want all of our citizen leaders and politicians to work as a team to benefit Americans. There will be no spin, but honesty and what is best for America. I am so tired of our side allowing the liberals and The Big Three to win and all we do is gripe! No more spinning wheels as we go into attack mode to expose the Democrats for what they are.

When all is said and done, more is said than done.

Lou Holtz

Each Generation Learns from the Previous Generation

I have been talking about this for a long time. I believe this should be a natural process that should be in all families. This happens when there are strong fathers that are role models and motivators. It is families that are all pulling together for individual success and encouraging all to be the best they can be.

It is imperative to learn from the triumphs and failures of earlier generations! This needs to be discussed in families so there will be less mistakes made in the future. Vice versa with victories in business, education, decisions, and life has to be discussed.

We have a major problem, because this is not happening and we see the proof every day. It is always somebody else's fault and poor me. There are the petty jealousies that are rampant in America. "Look! He has an advantage -- his parents are rich!" What these malcontents don't realize is that it probably took three or four generations for his parents to be in their position.

The great majority of Americans, when they came to America, were poor. There was years of back-breaking work and getting educated with degrees, skills, trades, and learning to use brains along with brawn. I am very proud of what my grandparents and parents have accomplished in their lives. I am now working my tail off and my son and daughter are doing the same.

Many of you are at the beginning or middle of this climb to success and you need not waver. Be persistent and keep looking ahead as there will be peaks and valleys. Get up every day and be ready for the challenge of life and always do your best to help those that want to help themselves. Be an innovator and motivator for all that you touch in your life.

Expect more from your family and keep raising the bar and always make sure you applaud all success!

If you are a single mother or father, stress the benefits of the family unit, mother and father. This is important because you have two people working together for a common cause instead of one person slaving on the most part and having many difficulties.

I plan on writing a Book about my time as a child working all the way to the present. I will go through the times as an employee, manager, and business owner. I will discuss opportunities and education. We will go through each stage and I will explain what occurred. I will be very blunt about my mistakes (many) and triumphs (not enough). I am an entrepreneur, so there will be a lot for me to share. Each chapter will have a summary. I will state what I did wrong and right and go into details. I want this to get done so I can perhaps help millions of people!

Summary

This is very important for the future of our country going forward and we need to change the downward spiral. Conservative Wisdom United will be a leader in this endeavor and we will push our political leaders to do the same. We need all Americans to look in the mirror and expect more from yourself and your family.

We want everybody to succeed. You know why? We want the country to succeed, and for the country to succeed, its people - its individuals - must succeed.

Rush Limbaugh

What is a Leader

A leader is the person who speaks up for the underdog when that person is right!

A leader speaks the truth and not all will like what he has to say, but is bold and will not back down!

A leader always leads into a battle!

A leader is not afraid of what others think of him, it only makes him stronger!

A leader will not compromise his character and ethics!

A leader is a motivating force that has others believing in him and his guidance!

A leader at times will raise a fist and his voice to make his point!

A leader will not allow others to walk over him or his supporters!

A leader will walk alone than walk with a crowd going in the wrong direction!

A leader is in a constant fight to defeat evil!

A leader engages with others and is always open for discussion!

A leader wants to help those that want to help themselves!

A leader encourages others to reach their full potential!

A leader will go into the lion's den and give his opinion!

A leader is fearless and is always ready to get after it!

A leader believes in the people and not a big controlling government!

Bob Brown

Conservative Wisdom United

8-4-2014

You have enemies? Good. That means you've stood up for something, sometime in your life.

Winston Churchill

The Media Left and Right Have Issues That Need to be Discussed

I receive my information from the far left to the far right. I also see it all in between and the slant, lying, and spinning. I am a conservative and I can tell you I can't stand our side not giving all the truth and not admitting to mistakes.

For example during the 2016 presidential election and after, CNN and Fox news it was day and night different. Really it is and was laughable because of what each network was not reporting and the spin was just terrible.

The major networks are big time criticizing President Trump and ignore or under report the evil and misdeeds of the liberals! Then we have Fox, Bloggers and Conservative Talk that are ignoring the lies of President Trump and still others that question him. Then still others that will jump off a cliff for him. Really all the press has lost its credibility and dignity.

I see conservatives that say, they want Juan Williams, Sheppard Smith, and Bob Beckel off of Fox news. Why do these people only want to listen to the news they want to hear? I don't think this is smart at all, and really the truth is it is really stupid. Keep your friends close and your enemies closer!

What I do is cut to the facts and the truth no matter to which side the axe falls on. I have been a big critic of President Trump and his strong followers and will continue to do so. The liberal left is the main problem and will be where I focus the most. The liberals are big on a huge government that controls the lives of Americans and all Republicans and Conservative will not agree to that.

Summary

I will be writing articles that will not spin and will be hard hitting. We will have disagreements on issues and we have to understand that is the American Way. My main discussions will be about the damage that liberalism is doing to our country and what needs to be done. I will in due time have other writers that will have a lot to say.

Conservative Wisdom United will create panic with the democrats!

Bob Brown

Americas Law Enforcement will be Supported Strongly by Conservative Wisdom United

This fraternity of brave men and women has been marginalized by liberal groups and The Big Three! We are going to stand with them in their time of need. They are out doing the dirty work that needs to be done to keep a civil society!

Unfortunately there are many areas of our country that are not civil and are contaminated by the unruly. These areas are primarily in our big cities that have been run mainly by the democrats for the last plus 50 years. Our officers in these areas see the lowest of life on a daily basis and they have to stomach the uncivil. The disrespect is rampant and our law enforcement has targets on their backs in some of these areas.

These areas are in the most need for police officers and they are the ones that treat the police the worse. If we would pull all law enforcement from these areas, and build a wall, they could not survive.

I do understand there are some bad apples that need to be picked. But what percent of cops are bad compared to people in the general population? I will take the cops by far, because we have a lot of Americans that are not up to par!

A prime example is the city of St. Louis which I am familiar with as I grew up and lived in the suburbs. The last 50 plus years has seen the criminal element expand their area to communities that were safe and sound.

I would love to see some of these liberals go out for a week with one of our officers to see what they have to endure every day! But as usual they will spin this with their typical PC and make excuses for the uncivil.

Summary

Our cops are going through a living hell because of the liberals. We all need to let them know we are on their side with a wave or a discussion. I do this all the time when I am out and I really love talking to cops and law enforcement. They need our support now more than ever!

"My heroes are those who risk their lives every day to protect our world and make it a better place – police, firefighters and members of our armed forces." Sidney Sheldon

The Strength and Respect For our Military Will be on the Front Burner

I am thankful that President Trump got elected because he will build up our military and raise the moral. Obama and the democrats are known for their dislike of the military and always do their best to handcuff them whenever they are in combat. The rule of engagement under Obama was a bad mistake and it created poor moral.

President Trump is very pro military and the moral with the troops will greatly improve under his leadership.

The most important thing for citizens to do for the military is to show your gratitude for their sacrifice. Many have been in the snake pit and some have not made it back.

I do this with law enforcement and our military, just a quick wave or in person, thank them for what they do! I love talking to them and hearing their story about life and what they have been through. Give it a shot they are very receptive to discussion and would love to hear from you.

Try this for a start with cops or the military, when you are out for lunch or buying groceries. Buy their lunch or slip them a few bucks for groceries and always give them a big thank you! Something this small will go a long way with them!

If you see a person or group burning the American Flag take action! Check your surroundings and motivate others to stand with you as you are going into the snake pit to rescue our flag. If you stand up that will give others the courage to stand with you! The alternative is to go in like our Fed Ex Man and take charge!

Summary

Our military needs for us to give them all the support we possibly can. They need to know that the great majority of Americans are in support of them and their families.

If you build an army of 100 lions, and their leader is a dog, in any fight, they will die like a dog. But if you build an army of 100 dogs and their leader is a lion, all dogs will fight like a lion!

Napoleon Bonaparte

Why don't we Help those that want to Help Themselves

I have an idea that may be able to help everybody that wants to live the American Dream. The first thing that needs to be done is to go back to my chapter (Each Generation learns from the previous Generation) we all need to understand this chapter and what needs to happen.

I believe if we concentrate on and set goals for the people in the middle class, it will help to bring everybody up a level or two. I think our government has been at least the democrats trying to keep Americans dependent on the government for all of their needs.

I think the mindset with a lot of young people that in order to succeed; you need to have a college education. I think this is true for many but with others this is not a smart move. The trades are looking for good help with no drug problems that will work and be responsible. Learn a trade and if you work hard you will always have a job and make good money. I have read a lot of articles about employers looking for help in the trades, machinists and so much more.

You need the mindset that you will take pride in your work and to look way ahead when you are a young person. Sacrifice a little with a part time job or small business that you can grow on the side.

It is an advantage to be married so you can have two pulling in the same direction. If not married and you are not making the money you desire, get a roommate.

I do believe that it is important to have a couple of things going at the same time. You need to always be thinking of different options because trends change and you need to be prepared.

What about shop class in our schools and home economics. We have to get people to start thinking and not what to think. Why not teach Entrepreneurship as a subject and have 1, 2, and 3.

Teachers need to push the D student to be a C student, and the C student to be a B student, and the B student to be an A student! The A student needs to be pushed with accelerated classes and maybe even skip a grade.

This is easier said than done because our schools are lacking and school choice is not the answer.

I think the people who are poor will see the middle class moving up the food chain, and they will get excited that they can move up to the next level. They all need to say to themselves, if he can do that I can too!

Summary

Don't feel sorry for yourself and pick yourself up every day and get after it. Pound into your kids that they need to do their best every day in and out of school. The work ethic and discipline is of the utmost of importance. Parents if your child is having problems in school, have him stay after or get him a tutor.

Everybody in America needs to say I want it and set your goals and reward yourself when they are attained. We all need to be motivators for each other and our families!

It is hard for entrepreneurs to borrow money, to start a project. We need the people who are doing well to offer to lend money at a fair rate or to even be a partner. The entrepreneur needs to show the money man his business plan and his ability to follow through. I know this first hand myself on different ideas that I could have used a few dollars. The need is out there folks for our inventors and people who think outside the box. I pray that I can be a lender to help others to reach their goals!

Republicans believe every day is the Fourth of July, but the democrats believe every day is April 15.

Ronald Reagan

A Democracy is Always Temporary in Nature

A democracy will continue to exist up until the time that voters discover that they can vote themselves generous gifts from the public treasury. From that moment on, the majority always votes for the candidates who promise the most benefits from the public treasury, with the result that every democracy will finally collapse due to lose fiscal policy, which is always followed by a dictatorship."

"The average age of the world's greatest civilizations from the beginning of history, has been about 200 years. During those 200 years, these nations always progressed through the following sequence:

From Bondage to spiritual faith; from spiritual faith to great courage; from courage to liberty; from liberty to abundance; from abundance to complacency; from complacency to apathy; from apathy to dependence; from dependence back into bondage."

Summary

Folks, this is something to give some serious thought.

Why Being a Conservative Republican is the Answer to America's Woes

The main difference between a liberal Democrat and a Conservative Republican is the liberals believe in a big government and we favor a small non intrusive government. We are all for the people and not wanting a big government to keep us down.

Conservative Republicans believe in free enterprise and waking up every morning with our goals. We want all Americans to be the best they can be and to live a long and prosperous life.

The feeling of working hard in school, work, and buying your first car and home with your own money is your reward. You need to have that fire in your belly and that get up and go energy to succeed.

You have to dream of success and a family that has the same desires. When a family member attains a goal, it is important to applaud them and encourage them to stay focused. We are optimistic people that always see the light at the end of the tunnel.

Conservatives believe in an expandable pie and the Democrats believe in a limited pie that we all need to fight over like scroungers.

The Democrat's desire is to have as many people on the government dole as possible so they can be controlled.

Capitalism and hard work is the answer and not the socialist ideals of the Democrats.

Summary

We all need to spread the word about the benefits of being a real Conservative. This is the answer for those who want the best chance to reach their goals. We need to make this our time and Americas time to understand that if you want the best for yourself, family and friends', being a Conservative Republican is the best way for all of us to go forward.

I hope we have once again reminded people that man is not free unless government is limited. There's a clear cause and effect here that is as neat and predictable as a law of physics: as government expands, liberty contracts.

Ronald Reagan

My commitment to Republicans, Conservative Wisdom United and Americans

I see an uphill battle Conservative Americans have in trying to get the car going in the right direction. I want to be in the driver's seat with millions of others that desire a Great America.

The Democrats are loading up and will attempt to sabotage, riot, lie and do whatever they can to knock us off the road. I believe they have awakened the Big Dogs that have been on the porch. They are now ready to get after it with bark and bite.

I am a strong Conservative Republican that believes in small government, strong military and personal responsibility. I will watch the Republicans and President Trump and will call them out when needed.

Our Super PAC Conservative Wisdom United will be up in the front battling the liberals and exposing their socialist views. We will be promoting Conservative views that are the best for all Americans.

Patriotic Americans I give you my word that I will always be up front and honest with everybody. There may be some hurt feelings at times, and then we all go forward!

Conservative Wisdom United

Bob Brown

Well, your greatest joy definitely comes from doing something for another, especially when it was done with no thought of something in return.

John Wooden

Super Pac Conservative Wisdom United

This is what it is all about folks us all working together for a better America for all of its citizens! I hope everybody enjoyed reading (Knock Out Liberalism And Keep Our Country Strong for All Americans) about all the issues we are going to be working on with our Super Pac.

I am extremely excited about our program and the potential to make the liberals irrelevant and to grow the Republican Party! I will need a lot of help with this endeavor with leaders, donors and supporters. My plate will be full as I will be going a hundred miles an hour all for our country. I want everybody to feel a part of our organization and have pride in what we will accomplish for America.

We will be visible year round with our billboards, charity work, town halls and so much more. This is how we are different with our work ethic and our money going towards our causes. A lot of Super PACs are heavy on administration costs and very little going towards action. We will keep our expenses to the minimum and I will keep everybody informed about what we are doing and our accomplishments.

I will be very hands on traveling across America to see Republican and Tea Party Groups. I will be looking for citizen leaders along the way and will be visiting a lot of businesses. Our billboards will be a very important tool that I plan to use a lot to our advantage.

Here is a little strategy that I will be using in the near future. Florida will always be a strong hold for us by the time we hit 2020 and beyond. One of my tools will be our billboards in chosen areas, and this is where I will need local help for placement. I will be concentrating on the Latino Community and I really wish I was fluent in Spanish. I will by this time have a lot of help in this area, because this will be a priority! I will see Republican and Tea Party Groups and will visit many businesses.

We will be concentrating on the Latino communities all across America because of our goal! I am a believer in setting goals and getting after it and I hope to mobilize others to be the same.

Summary

We are all going to work our tails off to knock the liberals out and to make them irrelevant! They are the enemy as they have hijacked the Democratic Party and all that is left are socialist that want to control American lives. We will not allow this to happen as the Big Dogs are getting off the porch and they will have bark and bite.

We will promote a Conservative agenda that is the best for America and we will motivate everybody to be the best they can be!

Be a part of Conservative Wisdom United and help better our country for all Americans!

There's such cultural rot taking place, such disintegration throughout our culture. Values, morality, you name it. Standards have been relaxed, and people are not being held to them. People's intentions, if they're said to be good and honorable, that's all that matters.

Rush Limbaugh

Get involved and be a game changer as a distributor and member!

Printed in the United States
By Bookmasters